the DOG's just been SICK in the HONDA
and other poems

Visit Colin Thompson's homepage at
http://www.atlantis.aust.com/~colinet
or e-mail him on colinet@atlantis.aust.com

A Hodder Children's Book

Published in Australia and New Zealand in 1999
by Hodder Headline Australia Pty Limited,
(A member of the Hodder Headline Group)
Level 22, 201 Kent Street, Sydney NSW 2000

Text copyright © Colin Thompson 1999
Illustrations copyright © Peter Viska 1999

This book is copyright. Apart from any fair dealing for the
purposes of private study, research, criticism or review
permitted under the *Copyright Act 1968*, no part may be
stored or reproduced by any process without prior
written permission. Enquiries should be made to the publisher.

National Library of Australia Cataloguing-in-Publication data

Thompson, Colin (Colin Edward).
The dog's just been sick in the Honda and other poems.

ISBN 0 7336 1007 2.

I. Animals - Juvenile Fiction. I. Viska, Peter. II. Title.

A821.3

Designed by Karen Carter
Typesetting and digital imaging by Bookhouse Digital, Sydney
Printed in Australia by Griffin Press, Adelaide

the DOG'S just been SICK in the HONDA

and other poems

Colin Thompson
Illustrated by Peter Viska

Hodder
Children's
Books
Australia

CONTENTS

Travel Sickness	7
Worms	11
Fish Are So Stupid	12
Arnold	14
The Dodo	16
Tiger, Tiger Burning Bright	17
I Had a Little Pet	18
I Had Two Little Pets	19
Flat Cat	20
Piranhas	21
The Best Pet That We Ever Had	22
Hickory Dickory Dock	28
Gerbil	29
I Had a Little Pet	30
I Had a Little Pet	31
The Dung Beetle	32
Doris and Maurice (and Horace)	34
A Fish	38
That's Not Very Nice	39
The Jellyfish	40
Humans Are Dumb	41
I Had a Little Pet	44
I Had a Little Pet	45
Can We Get a Dog, Dad?	46
Aristotle	50
I Had a Little Pet	51

Flick the pages from back to front to see the dog in the Honda

The Hungry-Bored-Cat-Fed-Only-On-Dog-Food's Dream	52
The Shortest Poem in the Whole World	53
Ants	54
Evolution	58
Tonsils	60
The Cleanest Cat in the World	61
Norman	62
The Bulldog	66
The Notwasp	68
Baa Baa Black Sheep	69
Slug	70
Extinct	71
The Silliest Animal Competition	72
At the Pet Shop	80
Humming Birds	82
I Took My Dog Swimming	83
Tadpoles	86
The Boy Stood on the Burning Duck	89
Vertigo	90
The Mayfly	91
Bob the Slug	92
Max	93
Bacteria	96
If	97
Noah's Ark	98

Travel Sickness

**The dog's just been sick in the Honda
And my dad says he's phoning the vet's
And if he lives to a hundred and fifty
We're not having any more pets.**

**The dog hung its head and looked guilty
Something went through its thick brain
Mum cleaned it up with some tissues
Then it turned round and threw up again.**

**Dad nearly drove up a lamp post
He screamed and threw open the door
We all got out onto the pavement
But the dog stayed inside and did more.**

Dad tore his hair and went purple.
Mum said, 'Don't make a fuss.'
And while Dad was having a breakdown
I took the dog home on the bus.

(Where it wasn't sick at all.)

WORMS

I got worms
I'll tell you how I got 'em
I didn't wash my hands
And now they're in my bottom.

I got medicine
Special stuff for germs
It tasted really awful
But it killed off all the worms.

Fish are So Stupid

Coelacanths
Can't dance.

Trout
Can't shout.

And stupid barramundi
Can't tell when it's Sunday.

Flatheads
Are fat heads.

A shark
Can't bark.

And stupid barramundi
Can't tell when it's Monday.

Arnold

I am a little budgie
Arnold is my name.
I sit and chirrup all day long
And have no claim to fame.

I sometimes eat a bit of seed
Or peck my cuttlefish,
Or talk to Arnold-In-The-Mirror,
Or paddle in my dish.

The highlight of my day is night
When they cover up my cage
And I can dream I'm flying free
And only half my age.

'Who's a pretty boy then?'
If I hear those words once more
I swear I'll beat my brains out
In the gravel on the floor.

I wish that I was in the sun
With a lovely budgie wife.
I wish I could escape this cage
And get myself a life.

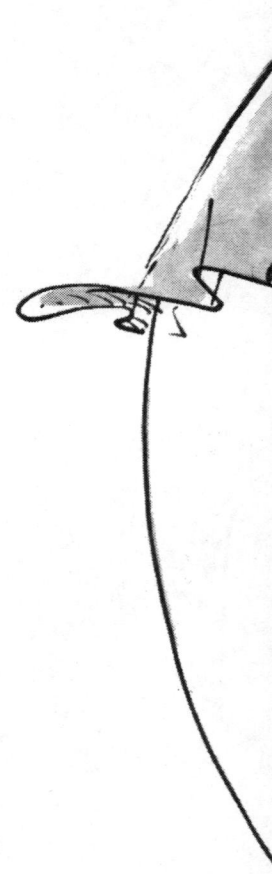

The Dodo

There was an old dodo called Fred
Who said, 'I'm supposed to be dead.
I'm extinct as can be,
I'm as dead as a me.
There's nothing else to be said.'

Tiger, Tiger Burning Bright

**Tiger, tiger burning bright
Who the hell set you alight?**

I Had A Little Pet

I had a little pet
A rather dull brown worm.
To make him look more lovely
I gave him a home-perm.

I HAD two Little Pets

I had two little pets
Both possums, both with lisps.
I fed them deep pan pizzas
And sausage flavoured crisps.

Flat Cat

**Dad drove over the cat last week;
He was old and deaf and fast asleep.
And so was the cat.**

**But poor old Pussy did not deserve
What he got when Dad didn't swerve.
And now he's a mat.**

Piranhas

Piranhas in pyjamas
Would be a lot more fun
Than boring old bananas
Let's hear it for P1.

Piranhas in pyjamas
Would like to play with you
And eat up all your arms and legs
Let's hear it for P2.

The Best Pet that We Ever Had

The best pet that we ever had
Was our old dog called Bert.
He hardly ever chewed things up
Except my grandad's shirt.

Well, he ate my coat
And the kitchen mat
And cousin Kevin
And next door's cat.

And the man next door
When he came to complain
But he threw him up.
And then ate him again.

And he never ran off
For more than a week
And he only bit people
When they started to speak.

And his breath wasn't bad
From a mile away
And we're hoping that one day
He'll learn 'sit' and 'stay'.

And he never did puddles
When he was indoors
Except on the furniture
And the beds and the floors.

And he was ever so careful
Where he left all his poo
He always made sure
It was under your shoe.

And we know he was sorry
When he chewed through the wire
That burnt down the house
In that terrible fire.

**The best pet that we ever had was Bert.
He didn't die
He just went off one afternoon
With someone walking by.**

Hickory Dickory Dock

**Hickory Dickory Dock
The mouse ran up the clock.
The clock struck one
Burst his eardrum.
Hickory Dickory Deaf.**

Gerbil

**What makes a little gerbil ill
Makes a caterpillar iller.**

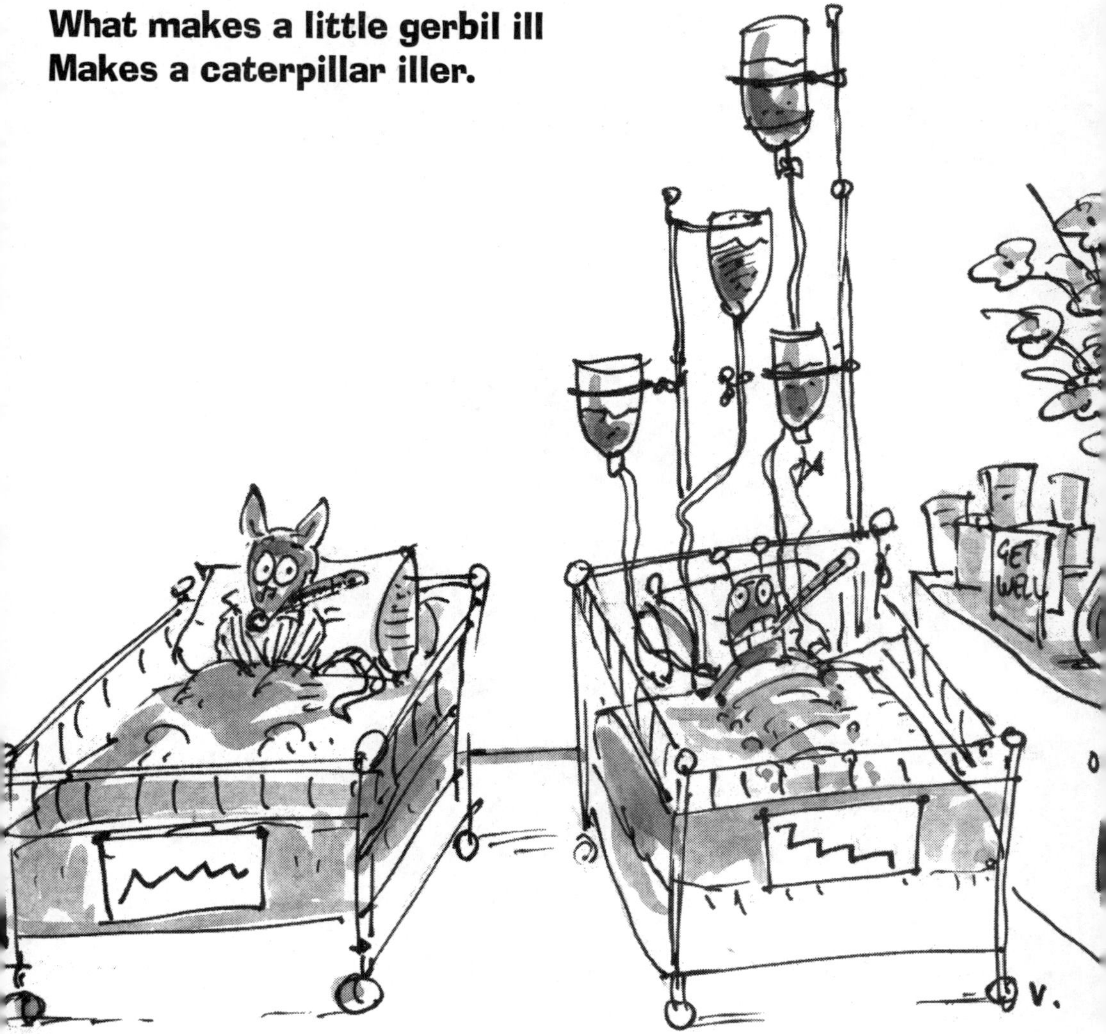

I Had A Little Pet

I had a little pet
A solicitor called Jim.
I used to fold him up at night
And keep him in a tin.

I Had A Little Pet

**I had a little pet
A crocodile called Roger.
One night he got into the bath
And ate my mother's lodger.**

The Dung Beetle

I am a small dung beetle
I live my life for dung,
Its praises they are numerous
But very seldom sung.

Dung is nature's bounty,
It's worth its weight in gold,
It keeps me fit and healthy
And cures the common cold.

I make it into bookshelves,
I wear it on my feet,
It's great upon the garden
And fabulous to eat.

It's all the same to me
From elephant or horse,
But best of all I love to eat
Dung beetle dung of course.

Doris and Maurice (and Horace)

**Doris
The Loris
Is incredibly slow
Due to a very small brain.**

**Doris
The Loris
Can't remember a thing
Sometimes, not even her name.**

**Doris
The Loris
Has a friend just like her
Except that she is a he.**

**Maurice
The Loris
Is in love with young Doris
And is trying to climb up her tree.**

**Maurice
The Loris
Climbed up the first branch
But then forgot why he'd come.**

**Maurice
The Loris
Like Doris and Horace
Is also incredibly dumb.**

'Is Horace
A Loris?'
I expect you will ask
'It's the first time that we've heard his name.'

He's a Loris
Like Doris
And Maurice the Loris
But to me they all look the same.

A Fish

I live in a bowl as round as the world
With some stones and a small plastic ship.
I swim round and round, then I swim back again
It's a pretty monotonous trip.

Last week I swam round and round for a while
And then I sat still for a bit.
And then I swam backwards just for a change.
I reckon that's about it.

THAT'S Not Very Nice

A bird flew by
Up in the sky
Except for the bit
That fell in my eye.

The Jellyfish

**The jellyfish lay on the beach
It was above the water's reach
Even at the highest tide.**

So it shrivelled up and died.

Humans are Dumb

**My human isn't very bright
In fact he's pretty thick.
Every time we have a walk
He throws away his stick.**

**He keeps on throwing it away
I bring it back again.
I think there's something missing
Inside his tiny brain.**

**He had a big red rubber ball
The nicest I've seen yet.
He kept on throwing that off too.
How stupid can you get?**

Sometimes when we're in the park
I can tell he wants a pee
But he waits and waits 'til we're back home
Ignoring every tree.

My human isn't very bright
It's something in his brain,
But he's ever so devoted
And I love him just the same.

I Had A Little Pet

I had a little pet
A wild filofax.
It hunted shrews and mice
And leapt upon their backs.

I Had A Little Pet

**I had a little pet
A clockwork mouse called Floyd.
Every time I wound him up
He really got annoyed.**

Can We Get a Dog, Dad?

'Can we get a dog, Dad?'
I ask every week.
Dad just goes red
And refuses to speak.

'Can we get a cat, Dad?'
I asked him instead.
But he just blew his top
And sent me to bed.

'Can we get a rabbit, Dad?'
I asked with a sigh.
'Oh sure,' Dad sneered,
'Inside a pie.'

'Can we get a fish, Dad?'
As the words left my lips,
I knew that he'd answer
'Yeah, with some chips.'

'Can we get a dog, Mum?'
I asked her one day.
'Not while your dad's here.
I'll send him away.'

'Can we get a dog and a cat and a rabbit and some fish and two budgies and a goat and a horse, Mum?'
'No problem,' Mum said.
'And while we are at it,
We'll get a new dad.'

Aristotle

**Aristotle the axolotl sat in his bottle and said,
'Life's OK, except that I'll
Be so much grander as a salamander.
It's a far more acceptable reptile.'**

I Had A Little Pet

**I had a little pet
A small wet slug called Trevor.
He had fourteen HSCs
But he didn't look that clever.**

The Hungry-Bored-Cat-Fed-Only-on-Dog-Food's Dream

The Shortest Poem in the Whole World*
(or the huge-bird-in-a-small-cage's dream)

I Fly.

*Unless you can think of one that's even shorter.

Ants

There's ants in my pants,
They're biting my bottom
And I haven't the faintest idea
Where I got 'em.

And now I've discovered
A bird in my pants.
I suppose it went in there
Looking for ants.

There's a cat in my pants
Which is really absurd.
It came in through the zipper
And is stalking the bird.

**There's a dog in my pants
And it's chasing the cat
And it's just bitten something
And it wasn't the cat.**

That's why I'm standing here
Without any pants.
There was no room for me
With that lot and the ants.

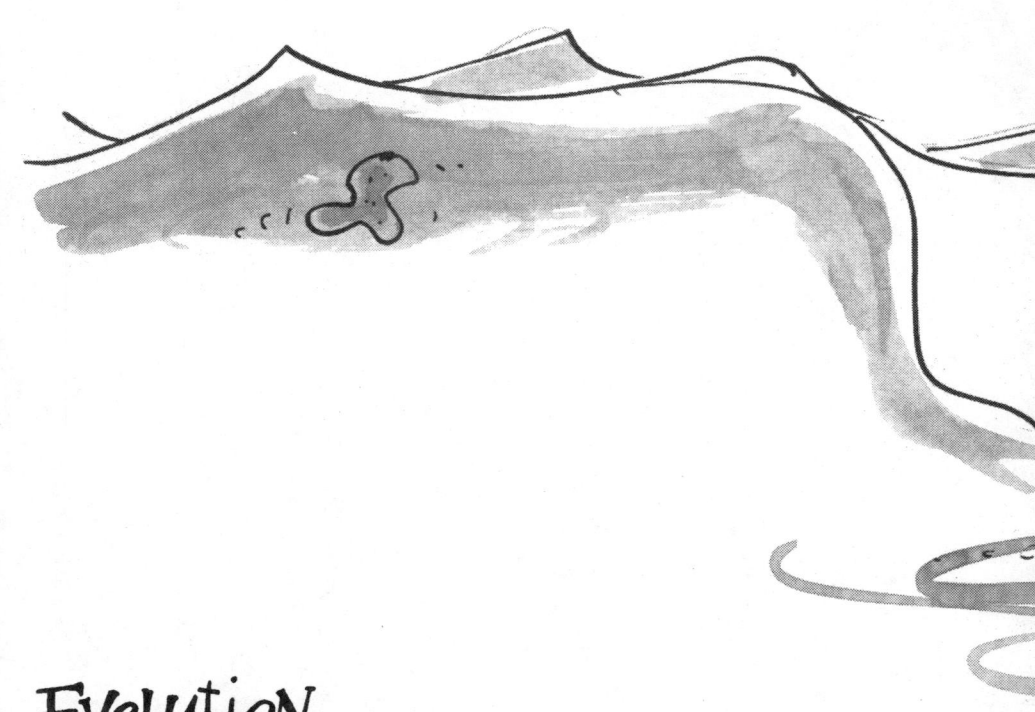

Evolution

A blob with no legs, no arms and no brain
Was lazing around in the sea.
For millions of years it kept changing a bit
And now it's become you and me.

Evolution's **OK** if you've plenty of time
But me, I want things to change now.
I want to be handsome and younger and rich
And I don't want to think about how.

You can keep all your work and studying hard
That's not how life ought to be.
I want to spend every day of my life
Just lazing around in the sea.

TONSILS

Tonsils sit inside your throat
And eat up all the germs.
Tonsils are disgusting things,
All slippery like worms.

Tonsils sit inside your throat
And watch the food go by.
Tonsils get all spotty
Then they hurt and make you cry.

The Cleanest Cat in the World

**Our cat fell asleep in the washing machine
And now he's the cleanest that he's ever been.
Don't try this at home. This has to be said.
For as well as dead clean, he's also clean dead.**

Norman

Norman the hamster escaped last night,
Got out of his cage in the pale moonlight.
Then vanished.

He ate a big tunnel right through the bread,
He ate both the ears off my teddy bear's head.
Then vanished.

He found Dad's computer and savaged the mouse,
He left chewed-up plastic all over the house.
Then vanished.

We got him a girlfriend to make him come back,
But he just released her out of the trap.
Then vanished.

The cat couldn't catch him, she just slept all day,
The dog was too scared and just ran away.
Mum shut her eyes and started to pray.
Gran just looked puzzled. She had nothing to say.

I went outside and started to play.
Dad's on a business trip off in Bombay.
Sis clipped the ends of her nails away.
Then varnished.

**So now there are hamsters all over the house,
They even released my sister's pet mouse.
Then vanished.**

THE BULLDOG

The bulldog is a funny dog
Both ends look the same.
This end is his bottom
And that end is his brain.

Hold on, no, I've got it wrong,
Or have I just forgotten?
That end is the head
And this end is the bottom.

The Notwasp

Granny's been stung by a bee
On her leg just above her left knee.
The bee stung her thigh
Then it flew off to die.
It wasn't a nice thing to see.

I wanted her stung by a wasp,
But nothing will rhyme with a wasp.
Not even a clasp
Or a gasp that you grasp
Though spelt right, will
Rhyme with a wasp.

Baa Baa Black Sheep

**Baa baa black sheep
Have you any wool?
Of course I have, I am a sheep
You stupid little fool.**

SLUG

**I am a little slug.
I feel so all alone.
If I was a snail
At least I'd have a home.**

Extinct

**The brontosaurus
Lived long before us.**

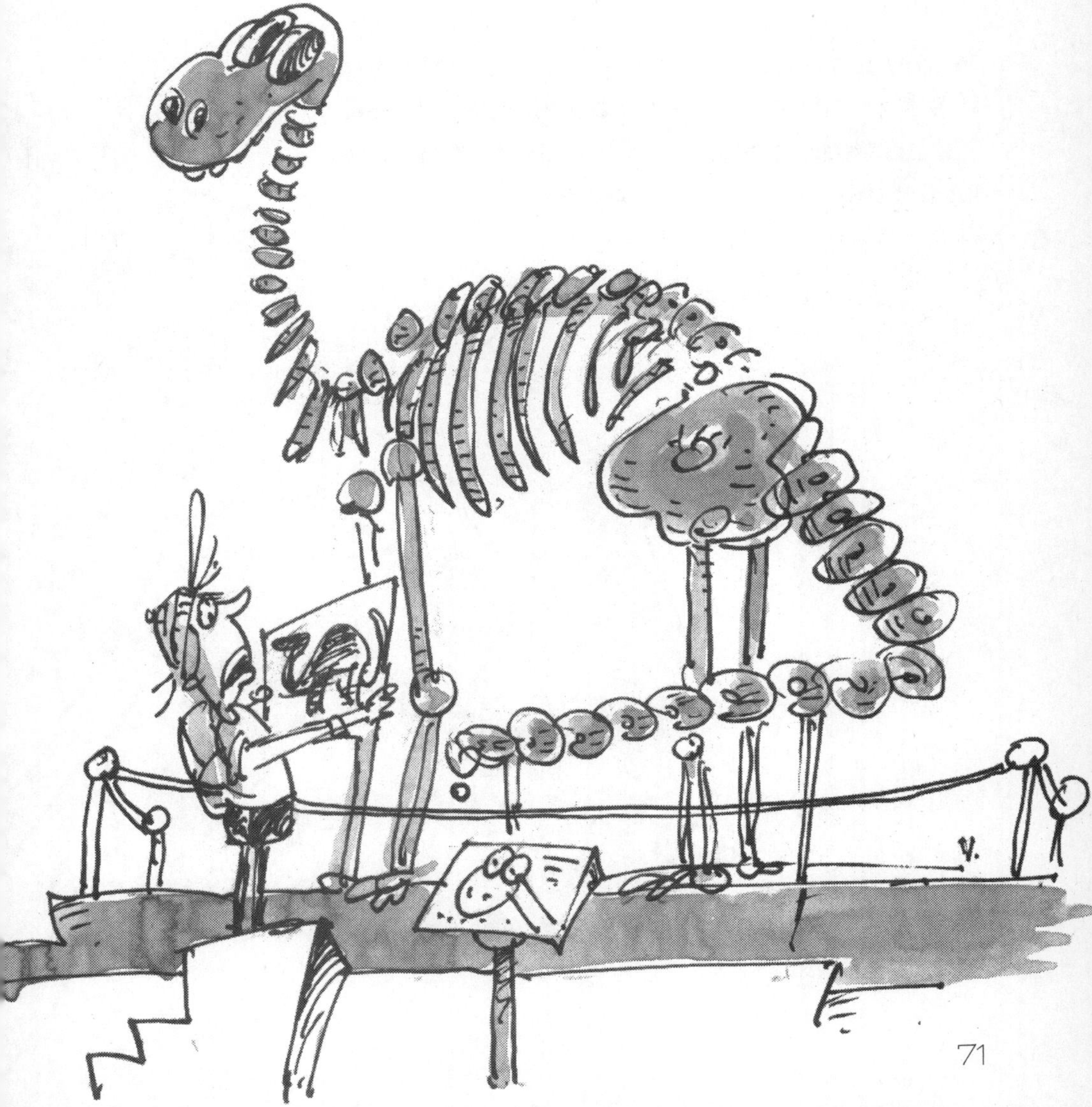

The Silliest Animal Competition

One day for a laugh, God made a giraffe,
He was bored making sensible things,
Like potatoes and bees and forests with trees
And creatures with beautiful wings.

Gabriel said, 'You've gone off your head,
It's the silliest thing you've made yet.
Its neck is a joke, it'll only get broke.
Everyone's bound to object.'

In all of the laughter, 'I could make something dafter,
I'll bet you,' said an angel called Clive.
So they all made a bet to see who could get
The stupidest thing to survive.

'It's got to survive, in fact it must thrive,
That's what the whole thing's about.'
So the old brontosaurus who was here long before us
Didn't count because he died out.

Someone put legs onto hard-boiled eggs
And painted their ankles bright blue.
Someone made chickens that flew underwater
But they ended up in a stew.

Gabriel's attempt was really unkempt,
All warty and covered with bumps.
'You've beaten the lot of us, with your hippopotamus,
Even the camel with humps.'

The platypus looked good, God knew that it would,
A furry thing swimming in water.
With a silly great beak, it was really a freak,
'If that doesn't win, well it oughta.'

Clive had a go with the useless dodo
But that didn't last very long.
'It just isn't fair, I'm getting nowhere
All of the best bits are gone.'

There was only a nose, two thumbs and some toes
And a horrible hairless behind,
Some bones and some string and a wrinkly pink thing
And some bits of old bacon rind.

So he chucked the whole lot into the pot
With anything else he could find.
Then he tipped it all out and gave a great shout,
'Hey, look I've invented mankind.'

God said, 'Nothing fits. It's all muddled bits.
It's the ugliest thing that you've done.
And as for that bit, though it may be a hit,
It'll just frizzle up in the sun.'

'Well, we'll dress them in trousers and bright
    coloured blouses,
That way they'll look even dafter.'
So God said, 'Right son, I reckon you've won.'
Sounds of cheering and lots of loud laughter.

At the Pet Shop

We went to the pet shop to get a new pet,
We couldn't decide what we wanted to get.
Jill fell in love with a tortoiseshell cat,
I said the puppies were better than that.
Mum said she wanted to buy a gerbil
And Dad was quite keen on the girl at the till.

Well, I got a labrador and Jill got a cat
And Mum got some goldfish and said that was that.
And Dad just looked moonfaced and said, 'That's not fair.'
So Mum went and got him a clip round the ear.

Humming Birds

**Why on earth do they hum
Those busy humming birds?**

**Because they can't remember
Any of the words.**

I took my Dog Swimming

I took my dog swimming down to the sea
Just past the sewerage drain
Where very strange things bob about in the water
And chemicals get in your brain.

My dog came ashore but his hair stayed behind
His knees were knocking and blue
Exactly the same colour you see in the water
When you hang those blocks in the loo.

His eyes looked quite wild with his tongue hanging out
There was froth all over his chin
And he kept on tripping and falling about
Like my mum when she's been on the gin.

The vet gave him medicine and three sorts of pills
But he threw them up on the floor
And no matter how much he pulls on his lead
He's not going swimming no more.

TADPOLES

We are a million tadpoles
Wriggling in the water.
Some of us are son
And some of us are daughter.

We are a million tadpoles
And we all look the same
And each of us has got
A millionth of a brain.

**I got fed up being like the rest
But I knew what to do.
I grew legs and hopped away
But the others did it too.**

We are a million frogs
Or maybe we are toads
And we're all getting squashed
By traffic on the roads.

We are a dozen frogs
Wriggling in the water,
Laying tons of spawn
To make new son and daughter.

The Boy stood on the Burning Duck

The boy stood on the burning duck
A stupid thing to do
Because the duck was roasting
On the barbecue.

Vertigo

**My budgerigar
Fell in a jar
But he didn't fall far
'Cause the lid was on it.
End of sonnet.**

The Mayfly

**The mayfly is the stupidest
Of all the little flies.
It hatches out without a mouth
So pretty quickly dies.**

BOB the SLUG

Bob the slug was fed up with lichen
So he crawled up the drain and into the kitchen.
He left a long trail of slime on the floor
As he wriggled across to the larder door.

He wriggled inside and climbed on the cheese
And dribbled a bit on some fresh lettuce leaves.
Then he fell fast asleep in a dish full of prunes
And got eaten by Dad and gave him the runes.

Max

The day I was born
Dad bought us a puppy.
Both on the same day
He said would be lucky.

We grew up together
Max was my best friend
On long summer days
That went on without end.

When I started school
He sat by the gate.
He was always there for me
Even when I was late.

Now we're both twelve
My life's just begun,
But poor Max's race
Is pretty well run.

It seems so unfair
That he's old and I'm not.
He got such a little
I got such a lot.

BACTERIA

**As pets bacteria
Are rather inferior
But they don't take much area.**

IF

If all the dogs in all the world
Were stood in one long line,
I reckon it would take three years
For me to pick out mine.

Noah's Ark

Long ago in the past in a far-away land
There lived a young chap they called Noah.
He looked at the clouds with his cap in his hand
And said, 'I'm not starting the mower.'

Then a voice from the skies gave him quite a surprise
When it called him by name and said, 'Son,
Don't bother to pack, but do bring your mac,
You've a helluva lot to get done.'

'I want you to go out on your patio
And build me a gigantic boat.
And although you may be many miles from the sea
When the rain comes you'll soon start to float.'

'It's only a shower, it'll be gone in an hour,'
Said Noah and God gave a laugh.
'My son, it will get so terribly wet
You will think that you're sat in your bath.'

Noah said, 'Me? But I'm stupid you see,
At school I ignored all the teachers.'
'Now listen, sonny, don't try to be funny.
We are going to save all the creatures.'

'Get some wood and some nails and some cloth for
    the sails
And a brush and some white undercoat.
And hurry up son for the storm's nearly come.'
But Noah said, 'Lord, what's a boat?'

At last all was clear but it took him a year
From the keel to the bunks for the crew.
Noah's wife said she'd rather instead
He'd built them a nice barbecue.

When the work was complete and looking quite neat
God said, 'Now go to the Zoo.
They've everything there, from gerbil to bear
And don't just get one, I want two.'

So when it was dark, Noah went to the park
And crept round undoing the cages.
Uncaged, the hyena looked quite a lot meaner.
To get the whole lot done took ages.

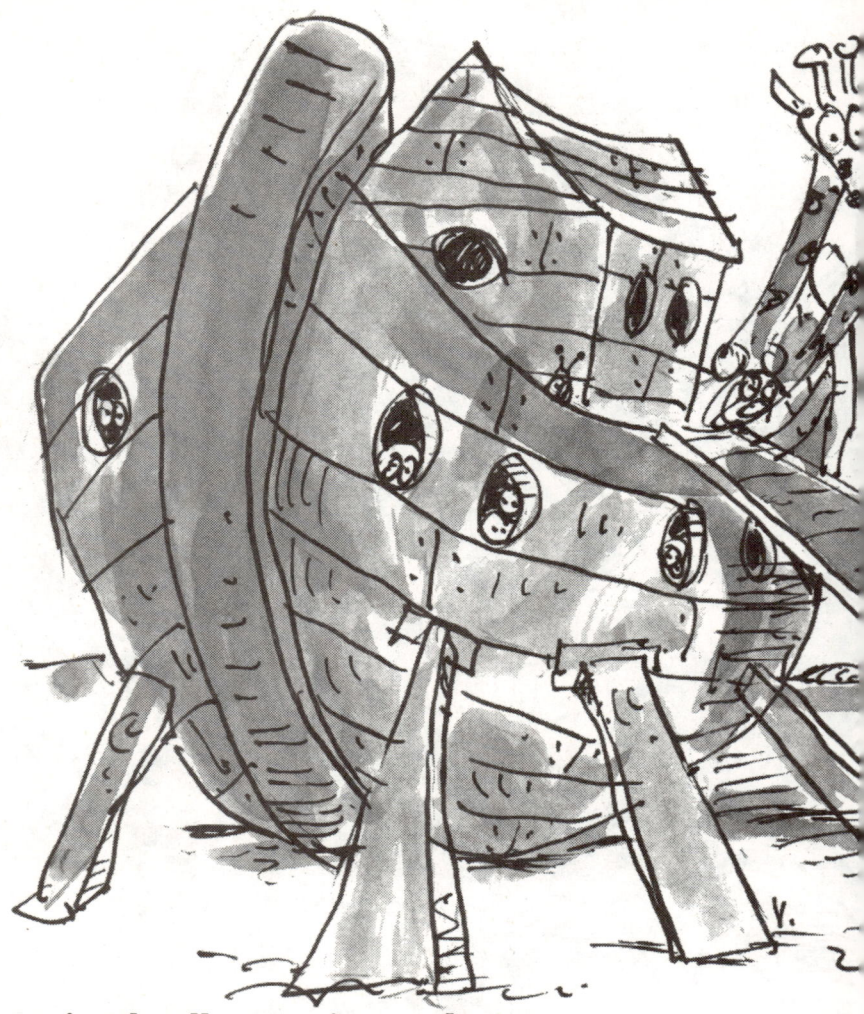

Then the animals all came in two by two,
The gazelle and the huge Bengal tiger.
When the lions came in, Noah hid in the loo
Where he sat by mistake on a spider.

From the tiniest worm to the huge pachyderm,
For several days they kept coming.
From the buffalo herd to the small humming bird
Who kept them awake with its humming.

**Then it started to rain and continued to rain
On and on forty days, forty nights.
Noah's wife, Betty, said, 'I'm going to bed.
I can't even dry my clean tights.'**

For day after day up in the crows' nest
The crows kept watch as they'd planned,
But all they could see was the sea like the rest
Without any sight of dry land.

They ran out of tea and they ran out of beer,
Noah smoked his last Havana.
'God help us,' he cried, but the Lord brought no cheer,
All he could offer was manna.

They finished the last of the old mammoth stew,
Had the sabre-toothed tiger on toast.
Ate bustards and yetis to name but a few
And finished with dodo pot roast.

'If we don't find land soon,' Noah said to his wife,
'There'll only be us and the rats,
And I'm not eating them.' So he sharpened his knife
And went off to look for the cats.

Noah said, 'Lord, we're all terribly bored.
Do you think you could please stop it raining?'
God said, 'Oh alright, I'll stop Saturday night.'
And on Sunday the land started draining.

On Monday a boy shouted out, 'Land ahoy!'
And the boat came to rest on a mountain;
But the water was slow and reluctant to go
So there wasn't much land to step out in.

But at last all the water went back where it oughta
In the ponds and the rivers and seas,
And back home in bed Noah lay there and said,
'All this rain has ruined my peas.'

'My shed's washed away and the carpets are grey.'
But his wife gave him reassurance.
'Don't worry,' she said, 'you'll get a new shed.
We'll claim it all on insurance.'